Forward Kirk Muller became captain of the Devils in 1987.

DEVILS

NEW JERSEY

BY ROSS RENNIE

CREATIVE EDUCATION INC.

Published by Creative Education, Inc.
123 S. Broad Street, Mankato, Minnesota 56001

Designed by Rita Marshall
Photos by Bruce Bennett Studios,
Frank Howard/Protography and Wide World Photos

Library of Congress Cataloging-in-Publication Data

Rennie, Ross.
　The New Jersey Devils/by Ross Rennie.
　p.　cm.
　Summary: Presents, in text and illustrations, the history of
the New Jersey Devils hockey team.
　ISBN 0-88682-283-1
　1. New Jersey Devils (Hockey team)—History—Juvenile literature.
[1. New Jersey Devils (Hockey team)—History.　2. Hockey—History.]
I. Title.
GV848.N38R46　1989
796.96′264′0974921—dc20
　　　　　　　　　　　　　　　　　　　89-37856
　　　　　　　　　　　　　　　　　　　CIP
　　　　　　　　　　　　　　　　　　　AC

THE BEGINNINGS: 1974–1981

When the state of New Jersey is mentioned in conversation, often it is not referred to in the kindest of terms. Located between New York City and Philadelphia, for many people New Jersey is just a place you have to travel through to get from one city to the other. Many people are unaware of the state's long history and vast beauty.

New Jersey stretches along the east coast of the United States, beginning north of New York City and extending as far south as Washington, D.C. The coastline is filled with

*Wilf Paiement joined the franchise in 1974, playing in both
Kansas City and Colorado.*

The New Jersey Devils were first known as the Kansas City Scouts.

magnificent beaches that provide a summer vacation delight for thousands of people each year. The northern part of the state is hilly and has some of the best parks in the country. There are numerous horse farms throughout the area and farming is still important to the state's economy. There are many reasons why New Jersey is called "The Garden State."

The state has also long been recognized as a place where education and research are important. Princeton University is situated in the heart of New Jersey, and Thomas Edison made many of his major discoveries while living in the town that now proudly bears his name. With that kind of history, and so much to offer, it is not surprising that many people have chosen to make New Jersey their home. With such a large population to draw upon, it's not unusual that there are many professional sports teams in the area. One of the most popular ones is the New Jersey Devils of the National Hockey League.

The club's history dates back to 1974, when the NHL allowed Kansas City and Washington, D.C., to join the league. With these two additional new teams, the league now consisted of eighteen teams in four divisions.

The Kansas City Scouts would eventually find their way to the Meadowlands complex in New Jersey, but not before they were reborn under another name. The Scouts lasted only two years. One need only look at their record to find out why. During those two years, the team won a total of only twenty-seven games out of a total of 160 played. It was dismal, to say the least.

There were many reasons for the Scouts' poor performance. As indicated earlier, the NHL had been on an expansion route for some time. The league had tripled in

The Devils of the late 1980s, featuring Patrik Sundstrom, beared little resemblance to the 1974 Scouts.

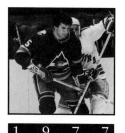

Menacing defenseman Barry Beck's aggressive play made him Colorado's first star.

size over less than a decade, and the demand for quality hockey players was bigger than the supply. To start a new club under these circumstances was a difficult task for anyone. Another major factor that inhibited the team was the creation of a rival professional hockey league in 1972, the World Hockey Association. Many cities that were not even considered for NHL expansion decided to join forces and start a new league. This only added to the shortage of quality talent in the NHL.

Although the team did not get much better after their move to Denver, the good news was that they remained in the NHL's weakest division at that time, the Smythe Division. In their first year in Colorado, the Rockies held a firm grip on fifth and last place in the division. For the third straight year, they failed to qualify for postseason play.

The 1978 Stanley Cup play-offs were the first time the Rockies qualified for postseason play, and their lack of play-off experience showed. Colorado's opponents were the Philadelphia Flyers. The Flyers had become the first expansion team to win the Stanley Cup back in 1973 and had repeated the feat the following season. It really was not much of a contest. The Rockies put up a good fight, but they were quickly eliminated. Despite their defeat, the Rockies had gained some valuable experience. Unfortunately, a decade would pass before the team would again qualify for the play-offs.

Over the next five seasons, there would be a new coach each year. No one, it seemed, could turn this team around. Lanny McDonald, the team captain during most of this period, did his best to inspire his teammates. But even the fiery McDonald could not bring the troops together.

By the end of the Rockies' fifth year in Colorado, there

was talk about moving the team again. The franchise was given one more year to prove itself. However, the task they faced was next to impossible. Never in the history of the franchise had the club scored more goals in a season than they had allowed against themselves. They had always lost at least twice as many games as they had won in any given season. Their dismal records also hurt attendance. With almost empty rinks, it was impossible for the NHL's worst team to even feel confident about home games. After their third last place finish in four years it was time for another move.

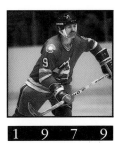

Team captain
Lanny MacDonald
did his best to inspire
his teammates.

Three gentlemen from New Jersey, Brendan Byrne, John McMullen, and John Whitehead, purchased the Colorado team and applied to the NHL to move the team to the New Jersey Meadowlands. The approval was quick in coming. A contest was started to name the new local team. Finally, the New Jersey Devils started the third life of a team that began nearly a decade earlier in Kansas City.

A NEW HOME, A NEW DIVISION, BUT NO CHANGE: 1982–1984

Just prior to the team's move from Colorado to New Jersey, the Meadowlands had its first sports team—the New York Giants—move into the complex. The Meadowlands provided easy access from the tri-state area, and the myriad of highways that surrounded the complex made it easy for fans to get in and out. The only thing that upset some of the folks was that after the football team moved, they did not change their name to reflect the fact that they were now in New Jersey rather than New York.

When the Colorado hockey team arrived, the club was

Aaron Broten led the Devils in both goals and assists during 1983. (pages 10–11)

Veteran Phil Russell's consistent, solid defense added to New Jersey's attack.

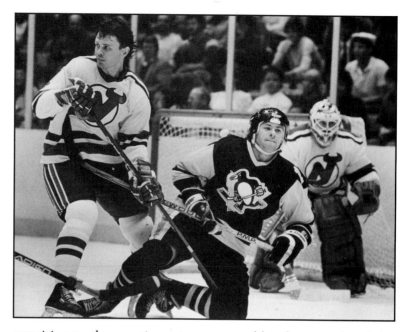

sensitive to the sentiment expressed by the people of the state. The team chose to use New Jersey as part of their name to help win needed fan support. It worked. Almost from day one, New Jersey's hockey fans—and many other people who had never seen a hockey game before—came out to support their local team.

The New Jersey Devils were placed in the Patrick Division along with the Pittsburgh Penguins, the New York Rangers, the New York Islanders, the Washington Capitals, and the Philadelphia Flyers. By the time the first season was over, it was clear that the Devils had not changed much from the Colorado team that had done so poorly. Not helping New Jersey was a change in the league's format. The NHL had changed the alignment of teams for the 1982–83 season and had also adopted the unbalanced schedule. The new schedule meant that teams within any division would play each other twice as often as they played other teams. With six teams in the Patrick Division, it meant that New Jersey would have to be better than at least two other teams within their division if they had any hope of reaching the play-offs. It was a difficult task, given the strength of the two New York teams, and the rest of the clubs in the division could be counted on to give New Jersey stiff competition as well.

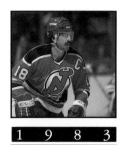

Center Mel Bridgeman joined the Devils, bringing his deft scoring touch to the team.

After a season in which the Devils had allowed 338 goals to be scored against them while only scoring 230, action was quickly taken to improve the team. During the summer break, the team acquired a tough center with scoring ability named Mel Bridgman. They also got Phil Russell, a rugged defenseman, in the same trade with Calgary. In a move to help ensure some success in the future, they purchased the American Hockey League's Maine Mariners franchise. This team would provide the Devils with a much-needed farm team to help develop their rookies before they faced the stiff competition at the NHL level.

Sometimes changes work and sometimes they don't. They did not work this time around. The 1983–84 season began poorly and never improved. After eighteen losses and only two wins, New Jersey hired head coach John McVie in an attempt to change the team's fortunes. McVie needed a miracle to turn the team around, and although he did his best, the damage had already been done. The team won fifteen more games that year under his command. That was enough to keep them out of the cellar, just three points ahead of Pittsburgh, but a healthy fifty-two points out of play-off reach.

Even though the team was a long way from qualifying for postseason play, the league's 1984 All-Star game

Kirk Muller was chosen as the Devils' first draft choice in the entry draft.

provided them with a taste of success. Two Devils were in uniform for the Wales Conference team. The game was played at the Meadowlands rink, providing a special treat for the local fans to see not only the best players in the league at one time, but also two of their own. And the Devils' representatives would have a wonderful night. Not only did Joe Cirella score a goal, but goalie Glenn Resch also was outstanding as the winning goaltender. It was obvious, perhaps for the first time, that there were some talented players on the New Jersey team.

More hopeful news came with the arrival of Kirk Muller, a promising center who had played on the Canadian Olympic team. Muller was chosen as the Devils' first draft choice in the entry draft that year. He would quickly play his way into the hearts of the New Jersey fans. In another move that would affect on the team's ultimate success, Tom McVie returned to coach the Maine Mariners farm team and Doug Carpenter was named as the Devils' new coach.

IMPROVEMENTS ARE SEEN: 1985–87

Opening night of the 1984–85 season would be a memorable one for several reasons. New Jersey won the game, but how the victory was attained was more remarkable. From the opening whistle, the Devils controlled the game. The New York Islanders were the opponent. New Jersey had not won a single game against them since moving to the Meadowlands. As the Devils piled up the goals, the fans yelled for more. They got more.

14   *Defenseman Joe Cirella was an All-Star in 1984.*

The fine play of Chico Resch and Dave Pichette (Page 17) improved New Jersey's record.

By the end of the night the team had established a franchise record as they scored seven consecutive goals without allowing a single one. It was magic! Even though the Islanders responded with two late goals, it did not matter. The New Jersey team had broken the jinx!

The loud cheers in the stands were drowned out by the chant that resounded, "Chico! Chico! Chico!" With that victory, Glenn Resch had recorded his two hundredth NHL win to become one of only twenty-six goalies in the history of the league to accomplish that feat. Adding to the celebration was the fact that the victory was Doug Carpenter's first as a new coach in the NHL. As the fans streamed out of the arena, they had visions of winning the Stanley Cup.

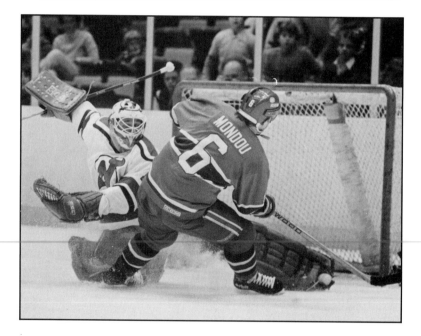

Rookie Kirk Muller was an All-Star in 1985.

Hard-working Pat Verbeek drew comparisons to superstar Bobby Clarke.

It would be a year to break jinxes. During the season, the team won its first game ever at the home of the Philadelphia Flyers, after losing twenty-five games without a win in the Spectrum. A few weeks later, the Devils traveled to the home of the New York Islanders and posted their first-ever win on the Islanders' home ice.

In late December, the team had a five-game unbeaten streak going and it really did look as if the franchise had some hope of not only surviving, but succeeding as well. Don Lever added some excitement for the hometown fans when he scored his three hundredth NHL goal. Fewer than sixty players in the entire history of the NHL had ever reached this plateau. Even better was the fact that the Devils went on to win the game over division rival Pittsburgh.

Unfortunately, when the 1985 season ended, the Devils

were only one point out of last place in the Patrick Division. But, more importantly, for the first time in their history, the club had almost qualified for postseason play. Carpenter had performed some type of magic. The team had finished only eight points away from qualifying for the play-offs, a dramatic difference from the Devils' previous season record, when they finished fifty-two points away from postseason play. The management was obviously happy with the team's improvement and offered Carpenter a two year contract. That may not seem like a long commitment, but considering that the team had seen twelve coaches come and go in the past ten years, it was a refreshing breath of continuity for the Devils.

1 9 8 6

Forward Greg Adams contributed thirty-five goals as the Devils finished last in their division.

TODAY'S NEW JERSEY DEVILS: 1988 AND BEYOND

Even though the Devils had improved their record year after year, it still was not enough to propel them into the play-offs. With stars like Aaron Broten, Kirk Muller, and Pat Verbeck on the team, it seemed as if the Devils should have been able to do better than their record showed.

When the team did not get off to a fast start in the 1987–88 season, coach Carpenter was replaced by young Jim Schoenfeld. The team would make some history under Jim, but most of the credit goes to a player acquired in March of that year. An untried goalie from the Canadian Olympic team, Sean Burke. His skill, some might say his luck, would make him an instant hero in the state of New Jersey. Burke recorded his first NHL win in a dramatic overtime victory over the Boston Bruins. That win would start an incredible turnabout that would propel the team toward its first play-off appearance.

Sean Burke was outstanding in goal during his rookie season.

As the season grew to a close, there were fewer than ten points separating all the teams in the Patrick Division. Even with an unbelievable nine wins and one tie in the Devils' last twelve games of the season, the final game of the season was the deciding factor.

In a closely fought contest, the Devils managed to edge the Chicago Blackhawks in overtime. For the first time in the club's history, the Devils had advanced to the Stanley Cup play-offs.

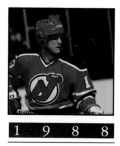

Center Patrik Sundstrom scored twenty points during New Jersey's postseason play.

They had finally made it; now the question was, would they survive? They had to face the New York Islanders in the division semifinals and they would need to win at least one game in the Islanders' home arena, the Nassau Coliseum. Game one was a heartbreaker. After New Jersey held off the Islanders for most of the game, New York tied the score and went on to win in overtime 4–3. The next night, Sean Burke took a much-needed rest, and the team rallied behind Bob Sauve in net to gain a tie in the series.

The team returned across the river to a welcome befitting a champion. This was the first time the Devils' fans could reward their players since their dramatic win in Chicago. The Devils responded to their fan support as Sean Burke recorded the club's first play-off shutout in the team's first play-off game at the Meadowlands. The 3–0 win gave them the lead in the series, a lead they would never give up. On April 14, 1988, before a screaming crowd that packed the arena, the New Jersey Devils hung on for a 6–5 win and a victory in their first-ever play-off appearance. A piece of history had been made. The team that Wayne Gretzky, in a foolish moment, had referred to as, "not really an NHL team" had made it to the division finals.

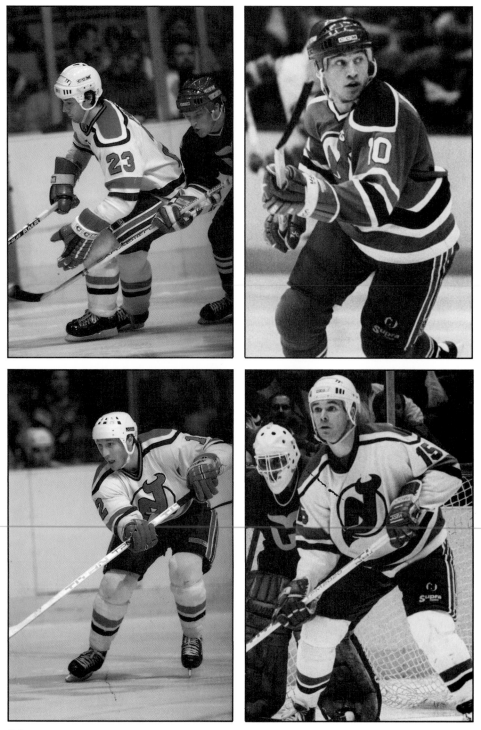

(clockwise): Bruce Driver, Aaron Broten, John MacLean, Pat Verbeek.

In that series, New Jersey's opponents were the Washington Capitals, the same team that had joined the NHL with the Devils back in 1974. It would be a memorable battle. Each team struggled during the series, both having trouble winning on home ice.

For the first time in team history, the Devils advanced to the play-off semi-finals.

The defensive style of the Washington team had made for a low-scoring series. It also made for a lot of close checking that resulted in flared tempers. In game six, while the Capitals skated to an unusually high-scoring 7–2 win, the Devils set an NHL record for the most penalty minutes by team in a play-off series.

When the series finally shifted to Washington for the seventh and final game both teams were exhausted. In a hard checking game the Devils outlasted the Capitals for an upset victory. Suddenly, New Jersey found themselves in the Stanley Cup semifinals. It was a thrill for everyone involved, especially the New Jersey fans who had waited patiently for so long. Could the Stanley Cup actually come to the Garden State? The Devils' fan club was sure of it. The Boston Bruins had other ideas.

The Bruins were the Devils' opponents in the Prince of Wales Conference championship round. The series began with the two teams trading victories. The excitement of the series was characterized by game three. When the Devils bowed 6–1 in that game, Schoenfeld made a critical remark to the referee Don Koharski. Koharski had made some calls against the New Jersey team that proved to turn the game in the Bruins' favor. The young coach was upset and told the referee in no uncertain terms. With the NHL's president away in Europe, the league's officials refused to suspend Schoenfeld. The storm of protest that followed

The capable Alain Chevrier won eighteen games during 1988.
(pages 26–27)

Center Kirt Muller
made his third
All-Star game
appearance.

eventually resulted in the refusal of any referees or lines-
men to attend the fourth game of the series in the Meadowlands. The contest was held up for over an hour as
amateur officials were obtained to handle the match. With
Schoenfeld behind the bench the Devils managed a 3–1
win over the Bruins to tie the series. However, this would
be Schoenfeld's last game of the year.

Due to increasing pressure, NHL officials suspended
New Jersey's coach before game five. The teams then
traded victories once more to tie the series and force a
seventh game in Boston. As in all final games in a play-off
series, the tension was nearly unbearable. The youthful
New Jersey team, without their leader behind the bench,
fell down 3–0 early in the game. They did not give up,
battling back to within a goal. The bubble finally burst.
Sean Burke could hold off the Bruins for only so long. The

28

Defenseman Joe Cirella was a key reason for the Devils' 1988 success.

Sean Burke notched nine wins during the 1988 playoffs.

The Devils slumped, despite the play of Aaron Broten, the club's all-time points leader.

Boston team went on to win 6–2 to eliminate the Cinderella team of the 1980s. Looking back it had been more than a good year for the Devils. It had been a great year!

When a team responds so well in a particular year, there is a lot of pressure on them to continue the high level of performance the following season. Unfortunately, the Devils were not up to the test. They hit a slump to end the decade once more in fifth spot in the Patrick Division, once again out of the play-offs. Sean Burke, in his first full season, had not been able to repeat his fantastic performance of 1988, and it was obvious that he would need some more seasoning.

For a team that had entered the NHL when it was nearly impossible to establish a winning club, the Devils have persevered for a long time. The team has survived two franchise moves and has discovered a potential for greatness. As the 1990s approach, they will strive for greater play-off success in hopes of achieving their ultimate goal —the Stanley Cup championship!